SPIT AND SPIRIT

SPIT AND SPIRIT

Pauline Beck

iUniverse LLC
Bloomington

Spit and Spirit

iUniverse books may be ordered through booksellers or by contacting:

iUniverse LLC
1663 Liberty Drive
Bloomington, IN 47403
www.iuniverse.com
1-800-Authors (1-800-288-4677)

ISBN: 978-1-4917-0675-6 (sc)
ISBN: 978-1-4917-0676-3 (ebk)

Printed in the United States of America

iUniverse rev. date: 09/16/2013

Contents

Companions on This Journey

Shared Seasons, Scenes, and Spirit

The Word's Echoing

To Father John W. Rebel
(February 13, 1937-March 17, 2013)

Introduction

This book was inspired and prompted into being by **Father John Rebel**, who told me for years that he was "still waiting for a copy of [my] book—a signed copy." He waited in this realm until March 17, 2013, when he was called home to the realm of the Spirit. I did not want him to wait as long in that realm to receive this book.

It has also been written for all the beautiful people with whom I've been blessed to share the wondrous journey of life: For my family and my friends, who have given me words, inspiration, encouragement, and, above all, love. For my sister Helen Erickson, who has been the mid-wife of many of these poems. For my brother-in-law John, who encouraged me to publish and answered all of my many computer questions. For my brothers Steve and Bill and my sister-in-law Beverly, who have reaffirmed in me the joys of nature and farming and living simply. For all of my professors in the English Department at Youngstown State University who awakened in me a passion for poetry. For Nancy McCracken and the Northeast Ohio Writing Project at Kent State faculty and fellows, who taught me so much about writing, sharing, and being. For my St. James the Apostle Parish family, who have inspired so many of these poems and have allowed me to share my poetry with them. For the Spirit that sparks all life and all creativity.

This is a collection of poems that bridge the space between this natural world of spit and that other realm of the Spirit. It is an expression of my experiences here and of my awareness of there. It is a gathering together of people

I've known, whom you've somehow known too; of events that have impacted my life and shaped my thinking and, in some way, yours as well; and of retellings of stories I've heard and read so many times—stories with which you are also probably very familiar. It is my way of swapping the spit and sharing the Spirit of life with you. It is my way of connecting to you and to the Source of the One Life that flows through all living beings. It is a gift given in gratitude for this life and for the blessing of all of you—both those of you who have come a long way with me, and those who are just now joining me on my journey through it.

COMPANIONS ON
THIS JOURNEY

Baptisms

(For Father John Rebel on his retirement)

He came to us as seasons changed,
in the bittersweet slipstream of summer,
at the first breath of the autumn
of his devotion to the priesthood,
with such young shoes to fill.

His head haloed with white wisdom,
his feet sporting sandals,
his eyes sparkling with spring,
he gathered all time into his present
and gave it generously to us.
He sang all seasons with his smile,
shrouded his sensitivity in sarcasm,
wore our hearts on his sleeve.

He was our Father, cradling us
in his strong, gentle hands at Baptism,
high-fiving us through childhood,
taking pride in our adolescent achievements,
being our guide through adulthood,
mourning our sad passings,
rejoicing at our sure resurrections.

He shared this blessed assurance
with his every word of comfort,
with his every warm hug or tender touch,
with his prayers and anointings.

He challenged us, cheered us, made us Church.

His quiet, quintessential grace
lived us into loving him
and longing for more time.

He's moving on now with his quiet grace,
in the bittersweet slipstream of another summer,
into a new season of life.
He's leaving us with his blessed assurances
that every ending is just a beginning—
a baptism filled with the challenge of change,
that love is the only constant,
that it outlives time's passing
and a loved one's moving on,
that it grows into the future
as we cradle one another in hearts
growing stronger and gentler with time.

He's fostered in us faith,
showed us how to hope,
gave us lessons in love.
"And these three things remain . . .
And the greatest of these is love."

Go Figure of Speech

In the magic, murky waters of the poet's mind,
mermaids made of dazzling words dive deep,
daring the darkness to silence their shining moves.
With flashing tailfins they fight against the fear
that lurks in the lurid pools of pathos and pain,
fight with the fiery passion of the poet's heart.

In the heat of these magic mermaids' thrashings,
all fears frizzle in the fire of fins and fiction;
and then the waters cool and calm themselves
in the quiet of the mermaids' meditations.
The poet plumbs these placid pools and pulls
from them mermaids morphed by memories.

Suddenly, in a surreal surrendering of the soul,
the poet finds a new voice singing a siren song
at the center of a serene universe unknown till now.
After an exhausting trial by fire and water,
the poet feels the freedom found in fins
and the absolute truth of the trope.

Flowering of Faith

My mother faced her fate with fierce faith and gentle grace.
She was acceptance in action. Like some fragile flower,
she leaned always toward the sun; and, even on her darkest days,
she always waited with such happy hope for its next rising.

In her glory in the garden, her beauty bloomed in the roses
of her blushing cheeks, flushed with the fervor of her efforts
to nurture nature, to love life into lush and luscious being.
She was the quintessential flowering of quiet motherhood.

My mother was that shy flower that bursts into blooming,
seldom seen, along some remote, rarely traveled road,
but such an amazing, astonishing delight to discover—
that shy surprise of splendor in the shadows of this world.

My mother faced her final hours with faith and grace.
In her growing weakness, she did not wither or wilt.
Leaning still toward the sun, she softly blossomed again
into acceptance through the blessed assurance of God's will.

Mother and Child Reunion

When I was born, you said I wore
a halo of soft, golden curls
around my fragile angel head.
You said you were reborn through me.
Each time you cradled me in your strong
mother arms, you felt my life
ebbing and flowing in your own veins.
You'd walk and rock and sing me to sleep;
we were one—joined at the heart.
You said you saw oceans in my eyes
and sailed upon them to a land
of purity and innocence and were young again.

Time raced on dragging us along for the ride.
Now, I'm holding the shell that once held you
in arms that strain against the breaking
of my heart. You smile weakly. In your eyes
I see clouds and a far-away land
that I can't sail to yet. You breathe
and in your breath I sense my own mortality—
a moment, a spark, a flash, a death.

Today

Today I saw my mother in the morning sun,
rising resplendent and warm with love,
chasing away the night and its dark heart.
I heard her gentle voice in the cheerful song
of birds, celebrating the birth of this new today.
I heard her words of comfort and encouragement:
"You made it through the night; today will be better."

Today I felt my mother's touch in the wind
softly brushing my hair from my face
and the night-dark fears from my heart.
I felt her kiss in the wind and the sun
and her love in the sweet embrace
of this day's dawning bright with hope.
I heard her words echoing in my head and heart:
"You made it through the night, today will be better."

Today I reached into the emptiness she left behind
and pulled out a million memories of moments
spent watching her love spring mornings like today,
watching her, like a child, watching life begin again,
seeing the joy of her heart shining in her quiet eyes.
Today I reached into my night-dead soul
and caught her Spirit in my trembling, reborn being.
I made it through the night; today *will* be better.

Peace Is Power

Knowing that fighting could never bring about peace,
he went to war unwillingly and unwittingly.
The draft dragged him from his family's farm
into the deadly dangers of duty for his country;
and he honorably discharged that duty,
laid down his plow and picked up their weapons.

Knowing that fighting would never bring about peace,
he was forced to fight in his country's show of force.
A humble young man, still in his teens, he forced himself
to become a "real" man and man a machine gun against men
he didn't know, even though he knew they were just like him.
Flying in the belly of a plane so close to Heaven,
he fought like Hell, knowing what he knew about fighting.

The Hell that is war swallowed him whole,
and in the belly of that beast he fought its demons
and was driven to distraction by the duty they demanded.
His gentle hands that could cradle with joy a lily,
or cup with love the chin of a child, fought with force
a people he knew shared with him One Spirit.

When the distraction disabled him for duty,
he was discharged, like Jonah from the whale,
back up on the shores of his land—his family farm.
He brought war back home with him, fought it again
and again in the minefields of his mind, trying to find peace.
Powerless, he fought until the day he died although he knew
even his fiercest fighting would never bring him ***any*** peace.

Buttercup Wisdom

Daddy would hold a buttercup beneath our chins
and tell us that if the yellow could be seen there,
that meant we liked butter. We believed him.
We would hold buttercups under one another's chins
and the chins of our childhood friends all summer long,
and now we hold them under our children's chins.
We tell them what the yellow stain means. They believe us.

Daddy shared with us so much of his life-taught wisdom
about the amazing wonders and miracles of nature,
about the mysteries and joys of living and learning,
about the powerful peace that comes from believing.
We drank from the chalice of his life-blood his sweet
innocence and incredible faith in a loving God.
We offer this chalice to our children now and tell them
that, if they eat everything on their dinner plates,
there will be sunshine tomorrow. They believe us.

Helen

(For my sister whose heart has been our school room)

Helen, the face that launched a thousand lives
from the safe harbor of her classroom:
her firm hands steadied the unsteady,
gave the cowardly new confidence
and the frustrated faith in themselves,
steered them with such tender toughness.

Knowing they must be made sea-worthy,
she readied them for risk-taking,
for facing sudden storms and crashing waves.
She taught them how to sound the depths
of their own minds and hearts and souls,
how to navigate the night of the world
by fixing their sights on the Heavens.

She commanded attention, affection, awe;
gave them nets of imagination and wonder
to cast into the living waters of being.
Master-teacher of her own fate and theirs,
she equipped their frail vessels
with sails strong enough to catch the wind
and take them into seas surging with beauty
and adventure and peace and love,
taught them how to fish for these,
gave their souls food for a lifetime.

Love's Laughter

**(For my brother Steve in whose heart God
has planted a garden that He continues to tend.)**

The earth is his great love;
he lavishes her with his life,
his time, from dawn to dark,
from spring to spring:
preparing, planting, tending,
harvesting, planning, preparing
again and again, year after year.

His garden is his delight;
he says he hears "God giggling
in the wiggling of the worms"
nurtured only by nature and his work:
harrowing, hoeing, tilling, healing.
His heart's in harmony with his hands,
the rhythm of his muscles:
the song shared by the soil and his soul.

There is no chemistry here, except
the one he has with the earth.
And many may laugh at this fool
who works from dawn to dark
in this day of DuPont and Monsanto,
but the only laughter he hears
is the giggling of God
in the wiggling of the worms.

Duet

(For my brother Bill whose heart and soul will keep singing forever)

Working from breakfast to bedtime
has whitened his hair, weakened his knees,
nearly broken his back; but it hasn't
silenced the song his soul is singing.
The song his heart sings in harmony with it,
with such love for the work that he does.

His heart and soul sing this song
to the beat set by the metronome
of cows' tails flicking away flies,
to the rhythmic whip and swish
of milking machines at dawn and dusk.
They sing it to the rhythms of the
combine's clicking in its picking
of grains of wheat or oats and sending
them in golden waterfalls of notes
into the empty, waiting wagon,
and the bailer's steady whine and clack
as it scrapes up loose strands of straw
or hay and binds them together
in blocks with cords of twisted twine
to the simple chords and the chorus
of his joyful heart-soul song.

His heart and soul sing it to the accompaniment
of his muscles and the music they make while
he works: milking, lifting, stacking, pitching.
They sing it to the accompaniment of instruments
his hands so nimbly play: rake, hoe, pitchfork.
His working from breakfast to bedtime
has drained some of his energy, but it hasn't
silenced this love song his soul keeps singing,
hasn't stifled the harmony of his heart,
hasn't stopped the flash-dancing of his dark eyes.

Wrapped

**(For my sister-in-law Beverly J. Beck
who is integrity and dignity)**

With her iPod filling her ears,
her skull, her soul with symphonies,
the soulful singing of whales and
the nightingale voice of Judy Collins,
she walks each day alone on the road
under morning suns on blue-sky days,
wrapped in the world whirling around her
as she passes green pasture grasses waving
in the breath of breezes that brush
her rose-garden cheeks as she walks.

Rapt in the beauty of the music of iPod
and life and the wonders whispered
by the wind in the woods, she walks away
her weariness, her weakness, her illness.
Moved by the music and the magic
of morning seen in the black-green
pines silhouetted against silver sunlight,
she walks giving thanks to the One Who
wakes her from darkness each day to live
with intense integrity and devout dignity,
to the One for Whom she pines in this life
she graciously receives as His gift to her,
this life she lives in love as her gift to Him.

A Voice Still Borne

**"So shall my word be that goes forth from my mouth;
It shall not return to me void, but shall do my will,
achieving the end for which I sent it." Isaiah 55:11**

Though you never got to
gaze on the cool green glory of summer,
or the orange, gold and scarlet spectacle
of a flaming forest in fall,
or the wonder of winter turning
an open field into a sea of white waves . . .

Though you never got to
listen to the soft music of April rainfall,
or the symphony of a July thunderstorm,
or the lonely song of December mourning doves . . .

Though you never got to
breathe in the freshness of country air,
or the scent of a red rose in full bloom,
or the pungency of spring soil, rich with decay
and ready to bring forth new life . . .

Though you never got to
taste the miracle of ice cold milk,
or steaming hot chocolate,
or the sweet of ripe strawberries or bananas,
or the brutal bitter of lemons or grapefruit . . .

Though you never got to
play, or sing, or dance, or dream, or laugh,
or cry, or suffer, or fear, or grieve . . .

Though you never got the chance to know
pleasure, or pain, or delight, or disappointment,
or wonder, or worry . . .

Though your voice was silenced
long before your first cry . . .

You awakened in us an awareness of the beauty
and the brevity of *all* these blessings of life
in this wonder-filled world;
taught us how inscrutable is God's wisdom
and how unfathomable are His ways.

Our minds ache with emptiness,
wanting more memories of you;
our arms, with wanting to hold you.
Still, our hearts must rejoice,
knowing that God's love spoke you into being,
then, called you back,
seeing that you had already achieved His will.

My Little Snicklefritz

When I'm at my worst and at the end of my frazzled rope,
you always manage to come wiggling your way in
like some slippery little eel; and my heart starts sniggling.
You come out of the shadows surrounding my day,
sniffling and grinning and wanting to play.

You come to me, my little Snicklefritz, when my whole day
is on the fritz, and I can't find faith in anything at all.
You fall into the moment of my deepest, darkest misery
like a shimmering star shimmying itself out of the night sky,
and I find myself beaming in the bright of your eyes.

When life has me up against the wall or down for the count,
I can always count on your nudging in and nuzzling next to me.
And I know then that angels do exist—wondrous, wingless ones
who cuddle close and keep the clouds from smothering me.
My little Snicklefritz, you always giggle me back to glee.

Little Wild Wind-Child

She's a dervish,
moving in madness
as quick as the wind.

One thing to the next,
her hands never stop;
feet barely touch floor.

Body electric
shocking my senses,
charging the whole house
where she is confined.

She laughs through the room,
makes a break for it,
bursts through the doorway,
flies into the yard.

I rush out after
and try to grab her,
to settle her down.

But just like the wind,
she will not be caught.

Fragile Fractivist

(For Susie Beiersdorfer and all diminutive dynamos who are dedicated to defending our earthly domain)

They say she's "flighty," a real flibbertigibbet,
fueled with passion and on fire with purpose.
Small in stature compared to their company CEO's,
she stands strong and ready to take on the tiger,
to face without any fear the corporate giants.

A diminutive, frail female David, armed
with the slingshot of spiritual truth
and stones of solid scientific facts,
she stands in the shadows of these giants,
undaunted by their wealth and social status.

She does battle in the corn and wheat fields,
where their minions of metal and mortar
frack the earth, crack her crust, tear through
her subcutaneous layers of soil and stone,
and shatter the shale: the rock of ages,
her backbone, her solid foundation.

She carries her signs, chants her slogans,
cries out a warning from the wilderness.
They mock her passion as if it were madness
and pay no attention to her wild rantings,
but try so hard to silence her with their lies.
Armed with weapons of wisdom and words,
she will not back down, will not back off;
she will not be shut down, will not shut up.

A tiny, towering presence, she scares them
with her windmill jousting and her mad wisdom.
In their Garden of Evil, where they sow seeds
of greed and plant their poisoned promises,
she grows louder and louder as she spreads
her message and awakens the apathetic.
In their fields full of weeds and woes,
she is a blessed asylum and an assurance—
a small, thriving Sweet Alysum.

A fragile fractivist, she frightens them.

Blonde Ambition: A Work in Yellow

(For Kathi Ramunno-Finney and *all* artists who never let their avant garde down)

The quintessential artist,
she's as ethereal as her aura—
her yellow glow of energy
that flows from her soul
through her mind and her fingers
onto canvas and paper,
into plaster and metal
and clay and wood.
As avant-garde as her art,
she sees her bizarre world
through saffron-colored glasses—
sunflower-splendid and dandelion-dazzling.

Every instant is inspiration,
a golden opportunity for recreating
the banana-bright beauty of being.
She takes life with a grain of sugar,
never taking herself too serious.
Her laughter, as spirited as the wind,
tickles the sallow-faced universe,
gilds it with her giddiness.

When the world gives her lemons,
she hugs and squeezes them
and drinks their bitter liquid,
as she drinks life, to the lees.
And as she drinks and delights in
and recreates this jaundiced world,
she smiles wide and says,
"I'd like more of the world
to be yellow."

Desert Dialogue

He goes to the desert to lose his self,
to shake the city, like dust, from his soul.
He leaves the crowds and his cares behind
to unwind and find his center once again
in the alone of blazing sun and burning sand.
He wraps the heat around him like a shroud
and dies to all that is of who he has become.

Here there is no He.
In the quiet of windless afternoons, he hears
a voice deep within his being, deep with wisdom
and the wonder of all life spinning a web of oneness.
In the silent chambers of his heart, he feels the voice
beating a rhythm that swells to a crescendo,
and he climbs the wave into a blue ocean of sky-music.

Here there is all He.

He hears himself mirrored in the desert's refrain
echoing its solitary truth again and again,
as wordless and as mysterious as a mirage.
He drinks its life-giving water like a child
thirsty from too much playing in the sun of self.
He drinks the cool, blue-ocean sky-music
and find his Self in all that sings the Spirit.

TV Evangelism

The TV evangelist pedaled his prophecies with one hand,
and held out with the other redemption and healing
for the poor sinner's spiritual heebic-jeebies and physical ills.
His image beaming like the sun, his voice booming like thunder,
he spoke with the self-assurance of a Chosen One.

And the poor, suffering sinner sat rapt in the shimmering
silver glow of a television-transmitted trance.
His soul, already perched at the pivotal point
between salvation and damnation, was being bandied about
like some shuttlecock between sanctification and sarcasm,
between deep believing and dark blaspheming,
between crying out for his cure and cursing the TV crusader.

The evangelist drove out demons, and cripples threw canes
across a spotlight-sparkled stage and walked again.
He offered such healing to the audience at home,
who could only watch, in the discomfort of their living,
the mighty hand of God healing his helpless, hopeless
children who had been stumbling in the shackles of sin,
offered such healing for a phone call and a "modest donation."

The poor, suffering sinner sat in his threadbare clothes,
mocking the miracles of the magnificent Man of God,
who spewed forth the Spirit like some human Fountain of Truth,
and then he quietly prayed for some other way,
and for the healing of the TV evangelist.

Disarming Forces

(For our veterans on Veteran's Day)

Risking body and mind to stand up
for the spirit of freedom,
soldiers, sailors, airmen, marines
left home, family, friends, fear behind.
Sacrificing safety and self,
they offered all they had and were
to realize the dream of democracy—
the vision of living in liberty.

Shaking off their individuality, they put on the uniform,
became one body, mind, and spirit—
one force fighting for Freedom's life.
Taking to the air and the sea,
to lands unknown, unsettled, unsafe,
they fought and prayed for peace.

With weapons of war in their hands,
they held hope for harmony in their hearts.
They watched towns destroyed,
lands laid waste, and friends die,
yet they kept alive the spirit,
the dream, the vision, the hope.

These soldiers, sailors, airmen, marines
have seen the ugliness
and heard the siren screams of war.
They have tasted the mud and blood of it.
They have touched the cold
of metal weapons and lifeless bodies,
and they have come home—with bright, shiny medals,
with dark, haunting memories, and with hearts still holding hope
that the harmony that is Heaven will someday come to earth,
that peace will prevail here,
that today's children will not need
to risk body and mind becoming
tomorrow's soldiers, sailors, airmen, marines.

Country Epiphany

She had known only the city,
the squat stone-gray company houses
on the hill above the row of steel mills
that belched their black into the blue
summer skies and sent graphite sifting
through the window screens at night
to gather on the kitchen table,
needing to be wiped clean before breakfast.

She knew the mournful night-whistle of trains,
carrying in the ore, the coke, the coal,
hauling out the shiny steel;
the drunken laughter and the angry shouts
of mill workers gathered on the street corner
after midnight, having just left the bars
where they drank away the day's drudgery;
and the curdled sounds of the sirens
of police cars sent to break up their brawls.

So when he married her and moved her
to the country, she was lonely and longed
for the loud life she had left behind.
She would wake in the middle of the night,
surrounded by shadows and silence;
and, lying still, feel stifled by the stillness.
She ached for the angry shouts,
for the noises that had nurtured her,
filled her past, and wove the fabric of her being.

Then, one night she heard his quiet breathing
in sync with her muffled heartbeat
in tune with her soul's singing in harmony
with the music of the universe's humming.

And just as night was about to turn into morning,
she touched him gently in the dark
and felt a spark of enlightenment,
found an uncommon peace in the pleasure
of his flesh, the stillness of him, and the shadows,
playing mute melodies on her heartstrings.

Her life was changed, and lost, and found.
In her newness she knew now
the grace of the gray dawn,
dancing around in the silent sky;
and that evening she discovered joy
and the promise of the Spirit
carried on the wind and on the wings
of a blue heron, landing
on a quiet lake on fire with sunset.

Pure Practicality: A Proposal

He told her there would be no magic:
no Heavenly music, no whistles, no bells;
only the two of them in a house
they would build with their hearts;
only the routine rhythms of everyday living,
the singsong of life and creation
and children's laughter filling the rooms
with melody and movement—the day-to-day,
in-and-out movement of being together.

He told her there would be no talisman
to ward off worry or sorrow or pain;
only the kisses, the holdings tight,
the holdings back, the forgivings.

He told her there would be no fireworks:
no colorful flashings in the dark;
only the shining of 60-minute bulbs
lighting their life, burning hour after hour;
and, at the close, only the soft glow
of candles in windows of the house
that had been built, had filled, had emptied;
only this candle glow reflected
in eyes as vacant as the rooms
once filled with the mundane
melodies of moments and memory-making.

He told her there would be no magic:
no ethereal music, no talisman, no fireworks;
only he and she building and growing together,
living and loving life day after day;
only he and she and an eternity of love.
And she agreed . . . that would be enough.

No Strings Attached

The salty air settles around us, seeps from our pores,
as we lie in the sand and watch the waves break
gently on the edge of this sun-soaked beach.
Side by side beneath the shimmering sunshine,
our happy hearts beat together in harmony
to the rhythm of the tide and the gulls cries.

The world disappears and there's only you and I,
lying side by side dreaming one dream.
Your smile holds me close and I smile too.
We are one now in this shared smiling,
one in our side-by-side lying in the sands
of time and tide and the true Spirit of Love.

The sunlight sparkles in your laughing eyes,
and mine reflect this sparkling and their laughter.
Our closeness is so much more than close;
it is the total, mystical, universal unity of life:
each of us, a puppet with no strings attached,
except the one that ties us together and to God.

Reckless

I want to ride helmet-less again
behind you in moonlight.
To reclaim my youth, my zest.
I want to hug your essence
and inhale the night-smell of you
and taste the thrill and risk
the road, the curves.
To lean with you, our bodies
synchronized, to roar of bike
and silent song of asphalt.
I want to hold you close.
To let your breathing amplify
my pulse, magnify my spirit.
I want to risk and thrill
and race against time and age.
To know the passion, to feel
the power, to throb and sweat
beneath a wild August moon
on a road that winds and surprises.
I want to ride reckless, trusting
you in control, shielding me again.

Silent Screenwriter

I sit on the sofa at four a.m.
watching mute tongues
of lightning lick the night
and awaken the sleeping sky.

The window flickers and flashes
like a silent movie screen:
black-and-white images,
but with no subtitles.

In a room charged with electricity,
I sit on the sofa,
a silent spectator,
charged with writing

my own dialogue.

My Soul Is Magenta

My soul is magenta,
but I dress in browns and grays.
My soul sings and dances
while I plod away my days.

My soul spins and sparkles,
but no one here can see.
They're too concerned with how I look
to see this inner me.

My soul already knows the truth
that my mind still tries to find;
it plays among the Heavens with God
and leaves me here . . . behind!

SHARED SEASONS, SCENES, AND SPIRIT

Mirage

In this mirage of bent light and shadows,
we swim in a consciousness beyond our knowing.
Small motes of matter, we dance in the darkness
of our own making to a music only the soul can hear,
making our own melodies, trying to matter more.

The solid ground beneath our feet falls away,
and all we hold dear, all we hold onto for life
breaks away and spills into this real illusion.
On the edges of eternity, we find our rhythm
and dare to dance away death's haunting dirge.

We find our own harmony and fill our seconds
with its song that plays its way into our days
and nights and writes the scores of our lives.
We believe we are the composers of our being
in this mirage of bent light and shadows.

Still in the vastness beyond our beliefs,
the Maestro hums the Heavens into a timeless
tune played forever for every heart to hear
here in this mirage of bent light and shadows,
in this darkness of our own making.

Mourning Breaking

Like ugly lumps of gray-brown clay,
they line the top of the porch railing,
their melancholy music melting
in the early morning-sunlit air.

Their song, their dirge, drifts in
through the panes of the bow window,
pouring like liquid loneliness
into my still, sad, sleepy heart.

They continue cooing, crooning
until they somehow sense my presence,
watching them, wide-eyed, from inside.
Their song is suddenly silent.

Then, in a wave of woeful notes,
the Spirit lifts their leaden bodies
into the bright blue morning sky.
They break into beauty like spring.

Wings that hid their startling splendor
spread wide against the serene sky,
lift them into palpable loveliness.
Their grace grazes the face of God.

Dancing in the Hands of Time

Listening in the Sunday morning silence
to the steady, rhythmic ticking of the clock
in sync with the beating of my heart,
I'm a child holding the hands of my father,
dancing at dawn, barefoot in the dewy grass,
feeling the damp beneath my soul's
two small anchors, tethered to the ground
by the gravity of life and loving
every magical moment, spinning
second by second, held in his strong hands.

His face, like my mind, is wide with wonder
at the recurring reawakening of the world,
at the mystical, metrical music of morning,
played by the hands of time on the strings
of our hearts here in the backyard of living.
I'm a small child again, dancing with Daddy
in the damp dew of the dawning of day.
My small feet tap out time on the wet ground;
my little hands hold onto his gentle, holy hands,
hoisting me into the timeless hope of Heaven.

Joy in the Woods

When I was a child, I would hear the woods
calling me to come in and play among the trees.
Their gnarled roots reached deep into the dirt
beneath my feet; their ebony columns, into the sky,
broken into blue bits and silver shards of sunlight
by their uppermost green, leafy branches.

I would hear the oak and maple trees thundering
a challenge for me to climb their rough trunks
high enough to dwarf our barn and troubled house
beneath my tiny, trembling feet and gleeful gaze.
I wanted to climb above the tough of life
into the joy of tangled branches, full of birdsong.

I would hear the voices of angels singing in the bees
to the breezes that mussed the deep green leaves
and made magical music only a child could hear.
I wished to join them in their happy, heavenly home
by ascending branch-by-branch those towering trees;
but, even leaping, I couldn't reach the lowest boughs.

Still I stood motionless, mesmerized and mystified,
watching the shadows dance like frenzied friends,
laughing in the cool shade on the hottest summer days.
I stood as still as the stately tree trunks in the woods,
silent and stoic, rooted and grounded, but reaching
toward that broken sky, full of joy and birdsong.

Oasis

A small, pale blue pool appeared in the cloud-dark desert of dawn,
an oasis of light, as I stumbled from sleep, still steeped in dreams.
A small pool of wonder, like light-water, glowed in the east
above the black pines lining the edge of the backyard—
stalwart sentinels standing at attention, waiting for day to break
the spell of night that conjured up this cool blue pool.

I stood at the window, rapt in wonder, and watched the pool
fill with blue-gray light and wash the night from the sky.
I watched it drown the sentinel-pines in its cool water
and color them deep-green as they stood perfectly still,
still knee-deep in the black shadows of the backyard.
I watched with heart wide-open to receive it's blue-gray grace.

A small pale blue pool appeared deep in my sleep-steeped being
and washed away my dark dreams like the pines it drowned
in daylight, in waves of watery blue wonder and brightening sun.
I stood, watching the oasis, feeling this morning's quiet madness
making me giddy in the sunlight rushing radiant and real,
flooding the desert of dawn with its gushing of graces.

Beauty on the Wing

Two beautiful butterflies with papery wings
of black and mingled shades of purple and blue
flutter about the yard, bring me to my knees
in the garden to watch them flirt
with the flowers, the air, each other.

I stare in the glare of morning sun
gleaming through their iridescent wings;
I'm transfixed by their bright beauty,
their delicate dance, their silent song.

Their movements make magic in my heart;
their performance is a prayer filling the air
with joy, with the luster of their love.

My psyche takes flight from the cool brown
ground beneath my knees into the warmth
of the azure sky on the wings of their prayer.

These two beautiful butterflies are
dancing, praying, flirting, making love
seem so possible in this world so in need
of the magic of their flickering wings
and such natural, innocent love.

Serendipity

Waking each day
to the serendipity of grace;
the room hushed
in the silence of an overnight
snowfall surrounding the house
with its soft cushion of cotton;
or swelling with a symphony
of songbirds singing spring's refrain;
or the melody of summer raindrops
tap dancing on the windows;
or filling with fall's
final notes written on the wind
blowing the blues through
the nearby autumn woods.

Living each day
with the serendipity of the Holy
Spirit's exposition in the blessing
of a blizzard of blossoms
cascading to the warming ground;
or the lush green of gardens
growing to yellow, orange,
purple, and red ripeness;
or the conflagration of trees
filling the woods and sky
with scarlet and saffron flames;

or the whispering of the winds
sweeping pure dove-white snow
into drifts of divinity.

Closing each day
with the serendipity of prayer,
of my silent soul sighing gratitude
for each moment of miracle,
for every bright benediction.

Graced

God's graces generously given
from the Father's fruitful heart,
unasked for and undeserved,
spilled out in soft spring sunlight
and the morning songs of returning birds.
In breezes breathing through cherry blossoms,
cheered to sweetness by the Spirit,
and the whole world
rich with resurrection.

Poured out by the Father's loving hands
in the silent green screaming of summer
and its red shouting sunsets.
In sable nights lit by the laughter
of the florescence of fireflies,
like sparks of stars caught in jars
and dreams of giggling children.

Cascading down from Heaven
in the singing of Autumn's dying,
in a chorus of chaotic color.
The forests and fields crying out in
a cacophony of red and purple and gold.
In earth's giving up its ghosts,
giving in to the Father's will.

Drifting down in the silence
of winter's wordless wonders,
in the stillness of snowy landscapes
and skies crowded with clouds.
In the dim beauty of death
and the promise of rebirth—
earth's eternal turning
in the Father's holy hands.

God's gifts so generously given,
unasked for and unearned.

Summer Mornings

Linen-crisp summer mornings:
lace cloud-curtains hung out to dry
beneath a pale blue sky
in cool breezes breathing in
through the window screens.

Dew-clean, deep green-grass mornings,
sparkling in dawn's spongy sunlight,
soft and surreal as last night's dreams,
drifting into the dragon-heat of day,
being devoured with delight.

Misty, mystical summer mornings,
waiting wistfully in the wings of night,
ready for flight into the unknown
hopes and promises hidden
beneath the happy wings of birds
and in their joyful songs.

Joyous, sacred summer mornings,
held out in the hallowed hands of God
with such love and grace,
held out with the Father's hope
that they'll be embraced
by all His jubilant children.

Splendid, spell-binding summer mornings:
these unwrapped gifts given freely,
waiting to open eyes and hearts
to the wonders of summer days
that drift swiftly into summer nights'
soft, sable dreams of summer mornings.

These Summer Days

These lackadaisical days of summer;
this childhood feeling of being.
Walking in its wonder, wild and free;
sweet, green grass beneath my feet,
rich brown mud between my toes.

Sprinting carefree with brisk winds
playfully slapping my face;
its fingers mussing my hair.
Falling flat in a field of wildflowers,
breathless in its breeze-blown beauty,
below a sky as blue as a lover's eyes,
watching floating cloud shapes and faces,
smiling miles wide—so close to Heaven.

Or failing to outrun the storm,
thrilling at tongues of lightning
licking the darkening day-sky,
charged with its sharp power,
searching still for rainbows.
Dancing in the driving rain,
feeling its cool kiss and tickle
on my sun-bronzed skin.

Trying to outrace the hours
running headlong into night,
chasing florescent flashes of fireflies
into the peace of sleep and dreams.

These delicious, delight-filled days;
the lusciousness of sun and mud;
the succulent serenity of surrender
to summer's listless serendipity.

Split

The summer sky was bright blue
and shimmering with silver sunshine.
Although that aura of warning was in the air,
we were only children, and we were playing
our summer day away in the backyard.

We were unaware of distant whispers
of thunder or the quickening of winds.
The blue sky's sudden blackout surprised us,
sent us a little too late scampering for safety
to our old, musty-smelling stone cellar.

Great knives of light split the darkened sky.
Mother Nature's split personality switched
from gentle nurturer, doting on her children at play,
to madwoman out to destroy her offspring.
We felt her heavy breathing as she chased after us.

Barely making it into the clammy cellar
before she hurled hail and more lightning bolts
into the yard where we had been playing,
we huddled together watching her furious flood
start to seep in through the stones of the cellar walls.

She had no pity, had no compassion
for her helpless, fear-filled children.
She raged like an aged lunatic around the house,
and we knew we could not talk back to her
or question the integrity of the Father.

Autumn's Amazing Advance

A late-August morning fills the air with fog and quiet.
The gray, gauzy mist mutes the green grass and leaves
slowly dispersed by sunshine and the wind's gentle hand.
The dawn breaks forth in a silent crescendo of serenity,
in music made of the many miracles of life's movement
from season to season in its wondrous, wordless score.

In a melody played so softly that only the soul can hear,
the summer voicelessly sings her bitter-sweet swansong.
Breezes carry the mute tune through the woods, waking
to find its bright green fading in the spotlight of the sun.
The grasses, too, give up their glory to its stunning shining.
Only the sensitive soul can see the beauty of the fading.

All on earth is slipping into the deep of autumn sleep,
and all of nature plays its muffled, melancholy dirge.
Still, within the heart, there is a happy, hopeful tune
marking time to each sweet metered beat of all of life.
In the stillness, a vee of geese startles the soundless sky
with a hallowed hymn to the holiness of living and dying.

Woods in Winter

No more placid place than the woods in winter.
Tall trees stripped to the bark stand stark against a dark sky.
Saplings, waist-deep in white, sleep beneath them.
Soft flakes grace the air sifting through tangles of branches:
Breeze-blown beauty borne on the breath of Heaven.
The woods in winter is a sacred haven.

There's no more peaceful place than the woods in winter.
Its quintessential quietude calls us in and calms us.
We can't resist its summons; all outside the woods doesn't exist.
Here beneath the naked boughs, we bow our heads in awe,
our breath escapes like incense rising in quiet praise.
The woods in winter is a sylvan sanctuary.

No more passive place than the woods in winter.
Its bright white wonder works its magic on our busy minds.
We give in to the stillness; all our troubled thoughts are forced
    to flee.
Here, beneath the seemingly deceased trees, we find pure
    peace.
In each death-breath of the winter woods is a wondrous hope.
In each kiss of the wind is a wish and a loving promise.

No more perfect place than the woods in winter.

We face our fears and find they are figments of our minds.

All our worries are wrapped in the shroud of winter white
and laid to rest.

Here, surrounded by serene silence, we have no need for
anxiety or angst.

With every passing moment that takes our breath away, we
breathe in

the peaceful assurance of spring . . . waiting in the winter woods.

Resurrection

When the woods reawakens from winter's deep sleep,
it shudders and shakes off its now tattered shroud.
The veins of willow branches and blackberry brambles
fill again with the ruddy surge of new life, flowing
like the stream set free from its frozen tomb.
The woods shakes off the shackles of death
with a subtle suddenness and sweet surprise.

Returning birds fill with their joyous songs the silent
spaces between death and life, between despair and hope.
All that is within the heart of the woods joins in singing
the sweet refrains of release from winter's rough restraints.
Spring dances in the sunlight on the water of the stream,
dances with delight to the mute music of the universe,
to the carefree choreography of the great cosmos.

The drab browns and grays give way to spring's green,
slowly give up their hold on the heart of the woods.
Pale-green leaves fill the space between earth and sky;
they flicker in the sunshine sifting in in silver shafts.
Buds bursting with excitement begin to blossom
into pink and white wonder, and the sweet scent
of nature's certain, blessed, baby-fresh rebirth.

When the woods reawakens from winter's deep sleep,
it shakes us from our drowsy dreams of spring.
It whispers its wonders into our weariness,
sings its truth into our trials and our tiredness.
At its first resurgence, its sure rebirth, we know
all that we need to know of death and life,
of the woods and all that dies and lives again.

Eden's Breathing

Beneath this green canopy,
I believe I see Eden's breathing.
I hear the Spirit speaking in the spring
sunshine sending shafts of silver light
through muted chartreuse leaves,
in the sweet, sighing song of the wind.

Within the walls of this sylvan cathedral,
I sense some strange serenity
in the stillness surrounding me,
some surreal serendipity stirring
somewhere deep within my being.
I know that I belong here in the woods.

Among the wooden columns of tree trunks,
I am so small and alive and joyful.
I am a child again in the company of giants
whose corrugated torsos tower skyward;
I look up in wonder and awe
into a tangle of branches and beauty.

Beneath me, the quiet, wild violets,
with their deep-purple voices,
join in the wind's soft singing.
And a chorus of rustling underbrush
becomes a part of the sacred song—
the eternal sung-prayer of the woods.

Here Eden's breathing frees me
from all fears and frustrations;
the Spirit's song fills and lifts me
toward a sky broken by boughs.
And I bow beneath this green canopy,
like a child in awe of these giants.

Essence

Today I heard for the first time this year
pussy willows purring in the woods near the yard,
and winter's wild, white stallion retreating
in thundering surrender to the hope of spring.
Suddenly something soft started stirring
somewhere deep in the dim dawning light,
and in the depths of my winter-weary soul.

A chorus of cosmic voices began singing
resurrection; rebirth reverberated in the pale gray
mists of this morning made for miracles.
My mute mind, mystified by the moment, listened
to the purring, the thundering, the singing,
echoing in my heart their essential message:
There is one Voice calling us all back to joy.

Today I heard that Voice for the first time
in the silence of my spring-hungry heart.
I heard it loud and lovely in the new-born morning,
in the pale, palpable purring of the pussy willows,
in the quiet thundering of winter's white retreat,
in the harmony of the cosmic chorus
that softly sings to life every single soul.

Ghosts of Grace

Ghosts of childhood haunt my mind,
make me want to find that time again
when I could run barefoot through
the dew-drenched lawn at dawn,
climb into a cherry-tree universe
of small, sweet, round, red worlds
and make their sweetness part of me,
or splash in a summer stream
laughing with its water
dashing over rocks
sparkling in the sun.

These ghosts that haunt me want me to wake
to make of every day a mystery
filled with moments of magic and miracles;
they call me to feel wonder weaving
itself into the fabric of my spirit.
They call me to feel something inside me
blossom at the sight of crocuses in snow;
to feel something inside me swelling
with the buds on winter-dead branches
coming back to life again;
to feel the surprise of a rainbow's magic
wand bent across a storm-dark sky,
or the first flashes of fireflies
in the black backyard in June,
or the fire works of art
the woods become in autumn.

These ghosts call me to life
to rejoice in the routine of living,
to thrill at the excitement of everyday,
to fill with the pure pleasure
of empathy with the earth,
to gorge on and glory in
the grace of God.

So Precarious

Life, so precarious.
Prowling in shadows,
howling into the night
on this precipice
in the diaphanous moonlight.

A heart hollow and hungry;
a soul unsatisfied.
Searching the silence
for a whisper of wisdom.
Tendons poised to pounce;
teeth ready to tear
into a fleeting truth,
eternally escaping capture.

Filled with longing and loneliness
and questions just out of reach,
too elusive to be asked;
the answers hidden in the asking.

Life, so precarious
in shades of dusk
and shadows of night,
dancing in diaphanous moonlight.

Stardust in the Wind

("Dust in the wind
All we are is dust in the wind"
> **—Kerry Livgren quoting a line from a book of**
> **Native American Poetry)**

If we could hear the voice of God
in the winter winds,
and the Spirit's speaking
in summer's soft breezes,
we'd know we're not
"just dust in the wind."

We are golden stardust
blown into the world
by the breath of Heaven.
Each of us is a bit
of glittering matter made
of the mind of our Maker;
each of us, a miracle
and a Messiah wafted
into a world gone deaf
to the Deity and blind
to the beauty
of our own Divinity.

If we could hear the voice of God
in every breath of our brothers
and the Spirit's speaking
in the sighs of our sisters,
we'd know that we're not
"just dust in the wind."
We're golden stardust
and God's glittering hope
for this dusty world.

Time Forgiven

Today, the child of yesterday and eternity,
takes its first breath and cries out of the darkness:
an infant day with infinite possibilities and promise.
Borne into the light on the wings of the Spirit
that knows no time but now and always,
knows they're one and the same in living,
holds in Its flight time's beginning and its end.

This child, this new-born day, delights the stars
and sets the sun ablaze with the fire of life
that's been burning since the Word was first spoken
into the dark abyss and chaos of non-existence,
and Creation filled the dismal emptiness.
The same fire is burning still in the dark
of dread and fear and despair, burning bright
throughout all ages past and all ages to come,
in every human heart able to free the mind
from the self-imposed imprisonment of time.

Today is the present and the past, the child and the parent.
This forever, born again with every dawning of the light,
with every spawning of the Spirit of Life, breaks
out in singing that touches every insightful human soul
shrouded in flesh in this realm of imagined reality,
invites every body and soul to be joined in the singing,
to know and to feel the joy of today's timeless refrain,
and to forgive time for drowning out its music.

The Turning

In an instant, the world will turn
itself around in the mind of the universe,
in a beat of the heart of Love.

In a flash, fear will melt
in the fires of the Spirit of Life and Passion,
in the crucible of Virtue.

In that monumental moment,
all that was will pass away and that which is to be
will come to pass, come to stay.

We will see, at last, clearly
what we had seen "as through a glass darkly;"
and all the shadows will fade.

The Truth that not even time
and our vain pride could taint or tear to shreds
will outshine the night of life.

The shadows of time and space
will no longer hold us prisoners to self and hide from us
the cosmic meaning of our essence.

The Word that spoke the world
into her first turning will whisper into full being all that lives
and breathes the beauty of Creation.

In the unspeakable shining of Truth,
the lies of life that blind us to Its brilliance will fly
like moths into a candle's flame.

The clock's hands will be tied,
and pride will slide from the collective mind
as it recollects the days of Eden.

And shame will be seared and reduced to ashes
in the stunning beauty of Earth's resplendent rebirth,
in that intense instant of her new turning.

Wisdom

Wisdom walks slowly, carrying the weight
of a lifetime of learning.
She has stored in her soul
treasures still untarnished by time.

Wisdom remembers with her heart
what her mind has forgotten.
Though they are clouded by age,
her eyes are wide open and see
clearly the wonders of this world.

Wisdom delights in every day.
She feeds on the bread of brotherhood,
drinks the wine of compassion;
and with passion she dances
with trees, grass, and flowers
to life's mystical music
and the Spirit of the wind.

Wisdom has traveled through times
of trouble and times of triumph,
always taking joy from the journey.

Wisdom walks slowly, but uprightly,
in the ways of righteousness,
in the way of the Lord;
and she teachers her children
by her example,
teaches them the way,
teaches them to follow
in her footsteps.

Solitude

There is something to be said for solitude,
for slipping away from society
and walking slowly into the desert of Self
to listen to the scarlet sunset's soft song
in harmony with the happy heart.

There is a special peace found in solitude,
"a peace that the world cannot give" or take away.
Only in solitude can the soul find this serenity,
quietly waiting in the shadows at the edge of night,
in the pre-twilight twinkling of stars' blinking out.

There is a wondrous mystery found only in solitude:
the mystery of oneness and eternity in life,
the ancient prophecies written by God's hand
on every human heart and mind and soul
still ringing true in every present moment of time.

There is a mystical speaking of the Spirit in solitude
that can't be heard above the day-to-day hubbub
of living and working and relationships.
Only in solitude can we see the fire of the Spirit
blazing in silence its universal, secret messages.

There is something said in solitude to every soul
searching in the darkness of the desert of Self,
something that speaks the Spirit's unspoken truth
in the sun's rising, red with flaming wonder
and the taste of wine and God's burning Love.

There is something rare found in the solitude of the desert,
in the alone that connects all of Creation
in some special, choreographed, cosmic dance.
There is no "I" or "me" in the desert of Self,
only "we" who are dancing to the Spirit's timeless music.

Futility

On this quiet, quintessential Sunday morning,
the birds are charging the air with excited hymns of praise.
The grass, wet with dew droplets, dances
in the dawning light to the music of the wind
and the soft, sensual singing of the Spirit of Life.

Waiting in the wings, Wonder waltzes
with measured steps into the spotlight of day.
Wrapped in scarves of sacred silence, Wisdom
hums some secret song she learned in the heart of Heaven.
The whole world hears the humming and spins
its threads of stories from its measured moments of time.

Life is bright with Sunday's spirited singing
and alive with the fire of a sanctified sunrise,
unfolding its glories against the backdrop of pale gray sky.
In this glorious explosion of harmony, I find
myself trying to write my synchronized mind
into a melody that matches the magic of this morning.

I try, but find Sunday's Siren song too strong,
too strange to set to the music of my weak mind.
My soul scoffs at my struggle to put into words the Wonder
that waltzes in the wings of the Spirit, sparkling with sunlight
and singing its wordless worship into the ears
of all who hear with eager hearts and ethereal minds.

Centered

Feeling fragile and frazzled,
I find myself fighting to face my fate.
No longer fraught with fears,
I unfold my soul to the summer sun.
My weakness and weariness,
slowing my journey to a wearing walk,
are no match for the mighty
weapons of faith, hope, and wonder

Within my happy heart, I hear
God's lyric-less love song softly playing,
hear the angels' awesome arias
echo in refrain the Lord's eternal promise.
There is nothing that I want;
all I need is to know that His gentle hand
upholds me as I stumble on,
lifting me and leading me by His light.

No longer bound by body,
my Spirit breaks forth in flight and soars
into the realm of pure reality,
into a time-less, space-less place of truth.
I hold out hope and my hands,
eager as a child, to grasp the Father's gifts,
to give to Him my small piece
of beauty set free from this broken vase.

A Stirring of Spirit

My spirit, weary of being confined within my mind,
tired of being tethered by truths I've been taught,
of being bound by the wrappings of warped wisdom,
beats its fragile, fledgling wings against the walls
of the cocoon of comfort I've created to close it in.
It struggles in the darkness to escape into the light,
fighting to find freedom in the fluency of flight.

Stirring softly in the shadows of my searching,
my spirit writhes in the silences between my thoughts
with a languid longing my mind has not yet learned.
In its wings are wonder and magic and miracle;
they flutter in the dark corners of my existence,
caught and held captive in the bell jar of my being,
like firefly-flashes on a stifling summer night.

My spirit, wanting to break the shackles of my self,
challenges the cherished beliefs my mind has built
to shield me from the burning blaze of its beauty.
It will not be bound and breathes its brightness
into the mute moments of my meditative soul,
beats its fragile wings there with such fierce force
until that butterfly beauty fills me with its light.

Storm at Sea

When my small boat is tossed about
on the stormy sea of life,
and I must choose which cargo to let go,
I will jettison the baggage of my mind—
my worldly thoughts, my intellect, my ego—
and safely guard my priceless soul,
the gift God's Spirit breathed me into life.

If the storm rages on and I am fearful
that my little ship shall be shattered
against the rocky shores of space,
or mired in the murky shoals of time,
I will abandon the anchor that drags me down,
cast off the lines that tie me to worldly treasure,
relinquish the rudder I've used to steer my own way
to the destiny that I've desired.

In that moment I will give in to the Wind,
the Will of God, and let It take me where It wishes.
Free of all I've owned, except my faith and trust,
I'll let the Mighty Wind wind up the loose ends
of my life, wrap them in wonder and awe,
and let the Great Navigator guide me home
and welcome back me to Heaven's harbor.

Glimpse

In that final moment,
I glimpse infinity in an instant.
In that last labored breath,
I embrace eternity.

In a swift shattering
of all that was of life,
I explode into immortality,
my arms spread wide with joy.

Suddenly my body splits,
sending my Spirit soaring,
released from its prison
into the depths of freedom.

I'm hurtled into Heaven,
holding nothing now of what was,
holding now a winning hand—
the holy Hand of God.

I step into the silent serenity of sky,
unclouded by sight, sound,
touch, taste, smell,
sensing only the subtle stillness.

And in that stillness,
unfettered and unafraid,
I know, at last, the wonder
of the Word . . .

spoken in silence.

THE WORD'S ECHOING

The Word

Before the beginning, the Creator was content to dwell in
    darkness,
content to be alone with the Spirit and the Word
while all around Him Nature raged
like some caged beast about to give birth.
Then, in His Wisdom and out of Compassion, the Creator
summoned the Spirit and spoke the Word
with absolute authority into the abyss.
The Word was Love, and the Love became Light.
And the pure, placid power of the Word spoken in the dark
brought Nature to her knees, and she submitted completely
to the Will of the One who called to her in her tumult and
    turmoil.

In that Light the Creator calmed the chaos, set boundaries
    for the Earth
and limits for the seas, the rivers, and the oceans
and set the sun and moon and stars to guide and govern them all.
In the Spirit, with the Word, He cradled Nature in His hands,
held her and helped her to bring forth life in all its forms,
in all its beauty, and all its splendor, all in the Spirit of the Word.
And the Creator embraced nature, nurtured her, newborn
    out of the night
of nothingness and the muddy epitome of endless emptiness.
Touched by the Spirit and the Word, Nature became one
    with the Creator,
and all that she came to bear bore His handprint, was His
    handiwork.

And when she had done the Will of the Creator and given
    birth to all His life,
she sat in the stillness, surrounded by the Light, and heard
    the Word
repeating in her whole being in the quiet rhythm of their
    united heartbeat.
She found at last her true place and her real peace in Him.
And in the serene silence of the seventh day, the Creator rested
in her arms and knew at last the profound perfection of
    sharing the Word,
of giving up His contentment and giving of Himself completely.

The Voice

At the Dawn, the Voice was heard
above the dark abyss and the troubled waters' swirling.
And the Voice was filled with song.
All Creation heard the singing,
and the sun, the moon, the stars
did the light fandango
on the dance floor of the sky.

The world waltzed out of the chaos,
and Heaven held hands with its dance partner.
Trees, with lithe limbs, and vegetation
swayed to the rhythms of the Voice.
Fish swam, birds flew, creatures crawled
and stepped to the harmony
playing in their hearts.

And the Trio was content to sing
to the earth and the sky and all that heard within them,
until the music turned to monotony.
The Three Voices needed a chorus,
needed not to sing its Love song alone.
Man was danced up out of the dirt
and soon asked for his dance partner.
Woman joined in, and the two began to sing.

Their song was part of the song of the Voice,
and the Voice was a part of their garden-variety Love song.
They were two soul singers
blending the rhythm of their heart beats
with the rhythm of the Voice.
And this Love song filled the earth and the sky
and overflowed the couple's hearts now
joined into One by the Love song of the Voice.

Children in Paradise

In the beginning they beamed with the bright
beauty of the source of their being,
mirrored the magnificent image of their Maker
and lived in happy harmony in the Garden,
holding hands and hearts open to God's grace.
They glowed with God-given glory.

Each day they walked in wonder and awe,
embracing each other and all of existence
with the enthusiasm of innocent children,
caring for all of Creation with cheerfulness.
They laughed with joy at the lavishness of Love
and with the satisfaction of selfless service.

Every dawn was a birth, brimming with blessings,
and every sunrise was alive with surprise.
They delighted in the generosity of the Deity
Who had designed and defined them,
Who danced them into each day's reborn light
and eased them into sleep and dreams at night.

In the beginning they did not know how much
they knew in feeling God's presence flowing
like a mighty river through the Garden,
through all of Creation and their own veins.
They wanted more; and, in their wanting,
they lost all they had been given.

Dumbfounded

In the dim light, he whispered in the silence,
thinking aloud of how he had no son to carry on
his priestly duties here in the Lord's Temple;
he recalled the prayer he knew no longer
could be answered—the time-worn prayer
he had grown old asking.

He saw a figure forming at the right of the altar
and, overcome with fright, fell to the floor.
Engulfed in the scent and the smoke of incense,
an angel assured him he had nothing to fear
here in the presence of God.

Gabriel spoke the answer to his now pointless prayer;
and he, filled with disbelief, responded with doubt,
and, mystified and mesmerized, was made mute.

She, his patient wife, waited for him at home.
Steeped in shame, she loved him more now for loving her
despite her barrenness, and in her old age.

When he returned and wrote for her the Angel's words,
she, too, was filled with disbelief and fear.
She almost laughed. But, then, she looked
into his eyes, full of years and doubtful hope;
and she believed and conceived and bore him a son.

And when he wrote down the child's name,
going against tradition, trusting the Angel's words,
his tongue was loosed; and he glorified God.

Change of Plan

This was not the way it was supposed to be,
not at all what she had expected.
She had been resigned to live her life
in obscurity and in obedience
to her carpenter-husband,
accepting and doing what her father wished,
trusting that respect would lead to love.

Then, the Angel's wings and the Word
whispered in the darkness of her room
dashed her plans, altered her purpose.
And when the Spirit's overshadowing
overcame her questionings and uncertainty,
she still could not fully comprehend it all.
She knew it wouldn't be easy.

She had grown used to the hurt in Joseph's eyes
before the dream drove it away;
but she could, even then, see the doubt
lingering in his gentle gaze.
How could he understand what even she,
transformed by the Spirit's touch,
found too surreal to be the truth?

But here, on the floor of the stable,
as he held her hand, kissed her brow,
as she held in her arms the Child of God,
the Light of the World, the Prophets' Promise,
it all somehow made sense in her soul;
and in the storeroom of her heart,
she started to keep such moments—
these mysterious, mystical memories
that unite her in the Spirit to all mothers.

In that hour of His birth she became,
was born again to be, the model for all women,
humble and obedient, the handmaid of God.
In the hour of His birth, she came to know
the grace of submission to the Father's Will.
She stored this knowledge in her heart;
it shielded her as she shared with Him the Cross,
sustained her until she was borne up
to share with Him the Crown
and the glory and the power of love.

Bethlehem Bound

With night coming on
and darkness surrounding
the two weary travelers,
they stop for a moment
on the road to breathe
and think and connect
the dots that led them here
on this strange journey
into the unknown,
with only trust to keep
their hearts from turning back.

She moans and sighs
into the silence of the sand
and the stars starting to startle
the midnight sky.
She is heavy with child
and sleeplessness and questionings.
He softly strokes her hair,
tries to ease her pain
and to show her his heart
full of love for her and the Child.

But with night now
surrounding them with black,
his doubts and questions
creep back into his tired mind.
He wants to stop, to change their course.
Here with a night-dark sky
hiding Heaven from his sight,
he wants to turn back.
Then, the star appears,
tearing wide open the night,
chasing off the shadows,
restoring his faith.

With night routed and the star's light
settling in, he kisses her head,
caresses her hands,
smiles his resolve;
and the two move on
toward Bethlehem.

"And the Word Became..."

The star startled the sky, parted the darkness.
The Word shattered the silence, spilled into the stillness
of the chilly stable, into the ears of its dumb beasts,
into the hearts of His mother and the father in mute prayer.
The Word sang into the hills, into the dreams of sleeping
    shepherds;
It sang them awake to wonder and wordless amazement.

The Word was whispered in the night winds, in angel wings,
into the soul of a wretched, wistful world, weary and waiting.
The Word chased the chill from the hillside and the hearts
that had held onto hope, believed in the promise of the prophets.
The Word wrapped Itself around the world, turning in time
to the beat of the Word's repeating, echoing in earth's emptiness.

The Word called out through the Cosmos, called out in the
    Child's cry,
called out in the mother's quiet smile, in the father's rapt
    astonishment,
called out in all Creation's age-old anticipation of this moment.
It sang across the star-stricken sky a song of promise and hope;
It sang from every lofty mountain and in the deep valleys.
The Word sang to some mystical melody, sang in the minds
    of the Magi.

The Word's song awakened the sleeping shepherds, roused them
from their dreary dreaming, filled them, at first, with dread.
Then, the Word caressed them, cradled them like children,
calmed the chaos of their work-weary souls, sang them to peace.
In the starlight, the Word led them to the stable and the Child,
led them to level ground; and they humbly bowed before Heaven.

The Word chanted the mystery of the Almighty,
made it known to mother and father in the murky manger,
to the oxen, asses, and shepherds standing silent in the shadows.
The Word was singing this mystery in their being and in all
    of life;
they heard It reverberating throughout the wretched world.
They rejoiced at Its refrain and joined in Its joyful chorus of
    Love.

Embrace

The Virgin Mother bends
to kiss His soft spot;
her parched lips drink
the pulsing of a promise.
Her "Yes" brings her here
with her carpenter spouse
to this Bethlehem stable.

Together they hold innocence;
a magical mystery
unfolds like a flower
in this moment of miracle.
Together they search His face
for a taste of grace,
an assurance, an answer.

Her eyes fill with star-shine and wonder;
her heart, made deep
for storing moments like this,
stirs with the fire of Love.
She holds them both close,
knowing nothing of what will be,
trusting in the Father's Will,
an angel's words, and them.

Tonight is theirs to breathe in.
Their shared Spirit dances
in the darkness to the music
of a universe exploding
in angels' song and earth's rejoicing.
United tonight in this cold stable,
they embrace their destiny,
their humanity, their divinity.

Not in a Mansion

Not in a mansion bright with candle light,
but here in a stable lit by one remarkable star,
the King-Child lies in the straw, surrounded
by sheep and cattle and the light of Love.

On a nearby hillside, shepherds are startled
from their sleep by trumpet blasts and angel-song
and news too wondrous for their minds to hold.
They stumble, half-asleep, to see the Child.

They mumble as they stagger down the hill,
their thoughts muddled, but their hearts clear.
Filled with wonder, they have no need for fear;
and all doubt is dispelled by the light of Truth.

Inside the stable the air is rich with humble splendor.
In the muted darkness a mother's smile lights the night,
and a father's gentle hands hold their infant Son.
The shepherds kneel and know at once His fragile power.

The oxen, ass, and sheep breathe softly into the shadows
something their shepherd-hearts have longed so long for.
They all are spellbound and silent; there is no room for speech,
only for the mother's smile, the father's love, and the Word.

Not in a mansion, but here in a stable, a Plan unfolds;
an ancient promise comes to pass. Time stands still.
Outside the stable, the star beckons three kings to follow,
leaving palaces and pride behind, to find God's quiet voice.

Redeemed

On the outskirts of Bethlehem, social outcasts
on a chilly hillside settle down to sleep
beside the sheep they keep for others.
Beneath the star-drenched night sky,
they drift off to their dreaming
that dispels the drudgery of their days
and the darkness in their hearts.
In the silent stillness, they sleep
steeped in dreams of blissful peace,
finding solace for their troubled souls.
Suddenly they awake to rush of angels'
wings and words spoken like a song.
Quaking in fear, they hear with their hearts,
ignorant and innocent as children,
the good news being sung through the night
only to them roused from sleep and darkness.

Without understanding the wondrous words
woven by the angel voices into their waking
and into the tattered fabric of their being,
they stumble in the chilled stillness
toward the star's streaming like liquid light.
Their eyes wide, opened with wonder,
their hardened hearts hewn by Heaven's hand,
they find the Child, swaddled in a glow
of glory, lying in the murky manger.
They fall to their knees, knowing now
the full power of love and trust and beauty,

seeing it in the frail Infant's face
and in the fragile faces of the two
who gaze on Him in glazed amazement.
They feel this power stirring in their shared soul,
feel the Child's innocence invading them,
feel His love laughing life into their hearts,
and His overwhelming JOY dancing out all darkness.

Their eyes alone speak for them the feelings
they never felt before this manger-moment.
And in that instant, they see themselves
reflected in the Child's quiet eyes,
see their hillside dreams redefined,
see their wretched lives reformed,
see their thirsting souls redeemed.

Out of Darkness

Swimming out of the darkness of sleep and dreams,
her mind, steeped in night and fear,
cowered in the light of the Angel's radiance.
She stumbled to her knees in the dark
and stared into the light of Love
shining in the Angel's eyes and words.

Confused and confounded she knelt silent as a shadow
in her familiar room, now so surreal,
illumined by the Angel's glowing glory.
Her ears at last focused and her mind finding solid ground,
she heard the proclamation of the Word
and was struck by Its gentle power.

"How can this be?" she wondered aloud in the stillness.
She would be the Mother of God, of the Son of God,
of the Savior of a world deep in the darkness of sin
and selfish disobedience.
She questioned, but she obeyed
and was lifted out of the dark into God's Love-light.

Again in the darkness of the three-hour eclipse,
she stumbled to her knees beneath the Cross.
She knelt steeped in the blackness of our sins,
keeping her eyes focused on His face.
She was struck by His glowing Glory . . .
the quiet, forgiving light of His Love.

Kneeling in the darkness of the shadows of the Cross,
she felt the curtain of her heart tear down the middle.
Suddenly, the darkness lifted and left her
holding His lifeless Body to her aching heart.
And in that instant of brightness and beauty,
she became the Peace, the Light, the Love
that was bleeding her into being.

Simeon's Sword

In the shadows at the roadside,
eclipsed by her Son's shining splendor,
Mary watched the cheering crowd
laying cloaks and palm branches in His path.
Her heart swelled with a mother's pride
melting in the warm glow of His meek majesty.

Her Son, riding on a donkey in the dazzling light
of sunshine and truth, made her smile again—
her tender, knowing, loving smile.
She wrapped herself around this moment,
stored it with so many other mystical moments
in the quiet depths of her blessed Being.

Here to celebrate the Passover with family,
she knew no blood would be sprinkled
on the doorpost of her storehouse-heart.
She hid her secret truths from kin
and waited in trusting wonder for more news.

In the company of family, she found comfort.
Reports of His teaching and His touching love
and the dangers of His divine dreamings
were carried in by friends and on Jerusalem's winds.
She stood stoic, stretched her faith
beyond the breaking of her heart,
hearing of His betrayal by His friends.

She calmly unclenched her feeble fists
letting go of every fragment of fear,
holding out hope, holding back a flood of tears
at word of His sacrificial scourging.
Her gentle Son's agony at every lash
buckled her knees, but didn't weaken her resolve.

She embraced His stripes with a mother's love.
She felt again and again the thrust of Simeon's sword.
Her Son's passion poured into her wounded self
at news of His conviction and sentencing.
In serene stillness, she drew into her head
every thorn of His crown and His people's mockery.

At the roadside again in silence, she met Him—
her Lambkin, her Baby Boy, her Life.
She almost crumbled beneath the weight
of His crossbeam and His heavy heart,
bursting with divine love, broken by human hubris.

On the hill of Calvary in the shadow of His Cross,
she was transfixed by His ghastly gaze,
transfused with His tranquil truth
shining through the betrayal and the pain.
She was set free at the sending forth
of His Spirit at the will of God,
and Simeon's sword fell . . . useless.

Pieta: Salvation's Song

She held Him again in her trembling arms,
and her mother-mind made its way back
to another time she had held Him
in the warmth of stable straw and
the wondrous glow of bright starlight,
surrounded by shepherds, adoring Him.

She heard again the angel's wordless song
echoing through her soul and the universe.
She remembered Joseph's hands holding hers,
stroking her hair, calming and comforting her
after cutting the cord, coaxing the first cry.

Her mother-heart, broken open now,
spilled its storehouse of memories.
How many times she had held Him like this,
rocking gently back and forth, crying inside,
kissing a fevered face, tending a wound,
brushing away tears brought on by children's taunts,
reassuring Him that He was "***divinely*** different."

She held Him closer now, in this hour
after the darkness and His death,
held Him close to her broken heart,
rocked Him gently in the glaring sun
after the total eclipse of the Light.
She heard again a distant, muted song
and Simeon's words of wonder and warning.

Surrounded by soldiers and a jeering crowd,
she had received His broken, bloody body
into her tender, trembling mother-arms;
now, in the aftermath of their fear and hate,
she held Him close, felt the fire of His love,
heard that song echoing in the stillness
of her soul and the silent universe—
that prophetic, promised song of salvation.

Cradled

Cradled in her arms, He felt firsthand the power
of human love, felt it flowing from her fingers
touching His cheeks, His chin, His fists, His feet.
He felt its power to replace fear
with an acceptance of an angel's command.

He saw it, too, in the smile of His surrogate sire,
saw it sparkling in the flash of his dark eyes,
saw it glistening in the tears of joy
running like rivulets down his rough face.
He saw its power to dispel doubt
and allow submission to God's will.

He heard it in the Spirit of life
whispering in the wind through the night air,
in the song of angels heralding His birth,
in the rejoicing of shepherds on a hill.

He knew it in His Heavenly Father's
words echoing in His heart,
knew it in the fire burning bright in His quiet soul,
knew it in the light that displaced the darkness
of the stable and chased the shadows of sin
from a world weary with waiting
for the promise, a savior, an answer.

And on the night of His birth,
He knew, too, that the power of this love
would be the grace that would guide Him
from her cradling to His cross,
would deliver the promise of salvation,
was the answer that the world
had always had, but never knew
until He was cradled in her arms.

This Hill

From here on
this hill, I see all of human history—
its inception in innocence,
lifted out of the earth by my Father's Hand,
spoken into being by His Voice,
sparked to life by His Spirit.

From here I see humanity parading through the ages—
too proud to bow before Him who spoke them into being,
too vain to bend to His Will,
too blind to see His Image in others
and afraid to see It in themselves.

From here I see all of humanity—
My brothers and my sisters, wandering
through self-made deserts of despair,
cursing the One Who sustains them
with manna from Heaven, with living water.

From here on this hill, I see all of humanity—
haunted by haughtiness and hatred,
with hardened hearts, blind souls,
deaf to the Truth of the Word.

From here on this hill, I see all of human history—
summed up in a jeering crowd,
then, gathered in grace in My Mother's gentle gaze.
From here on this hill, the prophecy of peace glimmers
in the loving acceptance in her eyes.

From here on this hill—
the hope of salvation . . .

Eclipse

Kneeling in the shadow of salvation,
she struggles to embrace her faith.
Myriad memories sail across
the seascape of her mother-mind.
She recalls her baby
born in a Bethlehem stable—
kissing His little fists,
holding His haloed head.

She returns to the temple in Jerusalem
where her boy begins His Father's work,
begins His journey to this hill in Calvary.
She feels again her terrified relief,
knowing what only she could know.

She sees once more His feet
walking the waves to calm and save
His doubting fishers of men,
His hands healing the blind and the lame.

She returns to Joseph's side
as he lies dying
and knows the comfort of her Son,
speaking of peace and eternity.

Now, in the shadow of salvation,
she sees His wrists and feet nailed,
His delicate hands broken,
sees Him thirsting and pleading
and struggling to embrace His faith.
She hears Him speaking
of forgiveness and promise and paradise,
hears His final cry,
watches His agonized eyes
go beyond the darkening sky.
And in the eclipse
it is finished.

Judas and the Resurrection

He had sat with Him at table, a disciple, a friend,
dipped the bread into the dish with Him,
drank with the others from His one cup,
knowing what he would do, not knowing any more.
In the dimly lit upper room, he avoided His eyes,
not knowing why, not wanting to know.
He felt the sting of the accusation, of His words
wrapped in sorrow and hurt and some kind of love
he couldn't understand, couldn't trust or believe.

In the dark of the garden, in the shadows
of the ancient olive trees spreading their
gnarled fingers across the face of Heaven,
his kiss sealed their fate in that instant.
In the torchlight falling on His face,
he saw reflected in His eyes his own soul
wrapped in sorrow and hurt and that love
he couldn't understand, didn't know or trust.
Something seized him by the heart, drove him
back to the Temple in remorse, in shame.

He confessed his mistake, his regret; but that kiss
had sealed his fate, bound it to His.
He threw the silver on the Temple floor,
tried to run away into the darkness of the night.
A silver moon cast shadows on the earth;
he ran from the devils dancing on the ground,
and in the dark corners of his troubled mind.
He ran from the devils of despair, ran until
the night, and all his hopes ran out.

In the pre-dawn gray, the devils had their way;
he tied the noose and threw it all away.
Then, in the shadows of Hell, he felt the stone
rolling away, felt the surge of life and love
more powerful than shame, more powerful than sin.
He felt the warmth, saw the light of His radiance
overcome the shadows, drive out the darkness.
In His eyes he saw his own soul reflected,
transformed by some kind of love that now
he fully understood in his instant of salvation.
He knew it now in the grace of His embrace.

Reunion

She steps beyond the clouds
whole and young again—
the mother who gave her life to Him,
the mother who held Him once, long ago.

His arms spread wide again,
this time to welcome her,
send a fleeting flash of memory
into her heart, now healed and happy.

Her arms delicately reach out,
touch His mind, set free a tortured thought:
These arms that cradled Him in Bethlehem
cradled Him on Calvary.

Her eyes fill with a lifetime of memories,
sheltered all these years
in the silence of her soul.
His eyes meet hers
and the memories melt
in the warmth of His loving smile.

Those last moments—so gruesome, so gory—
now give way to the glory of God,
Her Son shining, resplendent, radiant.
In one embrace all sorrow is erased;
and, together again, they rejoice
in the wonder of her "Yes."

Saul's Conversion

Double deep in darkness,
his heart hardened with hate,
his mind maddening with murderous thoughts,
Saul proudly persecutes those who've seen the Light,
dreams of destroying the Way,
believes he's bringing the Wayward to divine justice.

With papers from the high priests,
he sets out for Damascus to gather the scattered
sheep and lead them to slaughter.
Outside that city Saul is swallowed up
in a glow brighter that a billion burning suns
and falls face-first to the ground,
feels the dirt of the earth beneath and within him.

In the blinding brilliance, he hears the Voice—
a gentle Voice, full of light and loving mercy—
asking, "Saul, Saul, why are you persecuting me?"
Suddenly Saul senses something new,
something strange stirring in his soul.
He's the lost sheep, hearing the Shepherd's voice
softly calling him to follow Him in His Way.

Saul opens his eyes to darkness,
his mind and his heart to the Light of the Word.
Saul turns himself inside out and over to the Lord,
finds himself on the Straight road, praying and fasting.
Emptied of self, forsaking his sinful pride,
he regains his sight and his true soul
at the hands of Ananias, at the Lord's command.

Saul sheds the scales of his blind injustice,
takes on the mantle of peace and the mantra of love.
He takes up the staff and the cross of Christ
and leads the Gentiles to "the Way
and the Truth and the Light."

The Stoning of Stephen

Brimming with grace and bright with the Holy Spirit,
Stephen, alone of the seven who answer the Hellenists' call
to feed their widows, knows that no one lives "by bread alone,"
feeds them the Word of God and the Truth of the Son.
Witnessing to the life-giving power of the Word and the Truth,
Stephen follows in the footsteps of the Lord,
performs wondrous deeds and marvelous signs in His Name.

Knowing the Law and its fulfillment in Christ,
knowing the command to lay down his life and follow in love,
Stephen lives in the shadow of the Cross and the light of the
    Spirit,
works wonders among the people, and is betrayed.
He faces the Sanhedrin with the Angel glowing in his face,
God's Word burning in his heart, the risen Lord appearing in
    his vision.
He hears their false accusations, speaks the Truth that condemns
    them
and him, like the Master, "a lamb led to slaughter."

Brimming with grace and bright with the Holy Spirit,
Stephen stands silent outside the city,
stoically withstands the thrown stones,
bloody and broken, stumbles and rises
again and again and again.
He commends his soul to Christ,
asks Him to forgive those who stone him,
and falls finally out of the darkness of the world
into the Light and the Love of the Lord.

The Cripple

Borne up by friends, he daily comes
to the temple just to beg.
He cannot walk; he's carried there
but never enters in to pray.
The righteous ones pity him
and give him silver and gold.
He wants nothing more;
he's content to be the beggar.

Today all that he knows will change
when Peter and John pass by.
He looks to them for that pity
he sees in all temple-goers' eyes.
He waits for them to hand him coins
before they enter in to pray.
His heart sinks as he hears Peter say,
"I have no silver or gold . . ."

And, then, to his surprise, he sees
in Peter's and John's eyes
a look he's never seen before,
but somehow knows that it's pure love.
He hears the Name of Jesus.
It echoes in his heart.
It strengthens him, and he can stand
and walk and jump and praise.

He enters the temple for the first time,
praising God and witnessing
to God's mighty ability to heal.
He is transformed; he's not the same.
All that was is now no more.
The chains are smashed and he is freed
by the gentle, loving power of the Name.

Rebel ... lion

(For Father John Rebel: February 13, 1937-March 17, 2013)

He was a rebel from his youth,
a lion for peace and justice
in a world warped by war,
in a society scarred by segregation.
He chose the road less traveled,
knowing there would be no going back
later to follow the other.

He became the long-haired priest
who longed to bring the Light of Love
into the deep darkness of intolerance.
He chose to dive into the world's troubled waters
and swim upstream against a turbulent tide,
carried along by the counter-culture current
of Christ's teachings and Life.

He fought the Good-fight
with fists unclenched, arms wide open.
Traveling from parish to parish,
he walked softly and spoke gently,
wearing his heart on his sleeve—
like some patch awarded
for taking hatred hostage.

He was the consummate rebel—
flying in the face of the forces of fear.
He was borne up on Spirit wings,
but his feet were grounded in faith.
He challenged and charged us
to march with him into the Kingdom
that lies within every human heart.

He led us to believe that the New Jerusalem
is already here, waiting for us to realize.
He was a reserved rebel with a wry smile—
a candle that he put up on a lamp-stand
to light the way to the Holy City,
to confirm for us that "blessed assurance"
of the eternal life that he won at last.

About the Author

Pauline Beck is a former English teacher; she taught English in grades 7-12 in the Youngstown City School District for 25 years. She has a bachelor's degree in education and a master's degree in English from Youngstown State University. She is a Northeast Ohio Writing Project fellow and a Poetry Alive! seminar participant. She has had several poems published in *Ohio Teachers Write, No War, No More, Youngstown Poetry,* and *Mahoning Valley Poetry*. She currently lives on a 30-acre farm in New Bedford, Pennsylvania, with her cat Calpurnia and her two goats Pygmalion and Billy Budd, surrounded by the beauty and wonder of nature.